VAN HALEN
FOR UNLAWFUL CARNAL KNOWLEDGE

MANAGEMENT: ED LEFFLER/E.L. MANAGEMENT
EDITED BY KERRY O'BRIEN, STEVE GORENBERG AND JON CHAPPELL
MUSIC ENGRAVING BY W.R. MUSIC
PRODUCTION MANAGER: DANIEL ROSENBAUM
ART DIRECTION: KERSTIN FAIRBEND
DIRECTOR OF MUSIC: MARK PHILLIPS

ISBN: 89524-645-7

CONTENTS

CHERRY LANE MUSIC: THE PRINT COMPANY

EXECUTIVE: Michael Lefferts, President; Kathleen A. Maloney, Director of Customer Service; Rock Stamberg, Advertising and Promotion Manager
Len Handler, Creative Services Manager; Karen Carey, Division Secretary; Karen DeCrenza, Executive Secretary
MUSIC: Mark Phillips, Director of Music; Jon Chappell, Associate Director of Music; Steve Gorenberg, Music Editor
Kerry O'Brien, Music Editor; Gordon Hallberg, Director, Music Engraving
ART: Kerstin A. Fairbend, Art Director; Rosemary Cappa, Art Assistant
PRODUCTION: Daniel Rosenbaum, Production Manager; James Piacentino, Production Coordinator

TABLATURE EXPLANATION

TABLATURE: A six-line staff that graphically represents the guitar fingerboard, with the top line indicating the highest sounding string (high E). By placing a number on the appropriate line, the string and fret of any note can be indicated. The number 0 represents an open string.

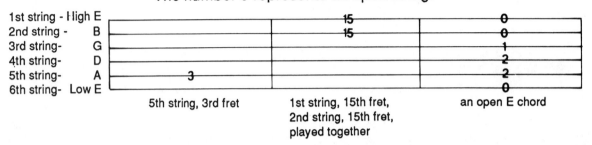

1st string - High E
2nd string - B
3rd string - G
4th string - D
5th string - A
6th string - Low E

5th string, 3rd fret   1st string, 15th fret,   an open E chord
                              2nd string, 15th fret,
                              played together

Definitions for Special Guitar Notation

BEND: Strike the note and bend up ½ step (one fret).

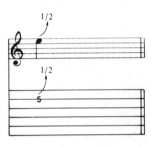

BEND: Strike the note and bend up a whole step (two frets).

BEND AND RELEASE: Strike the note and bend up ½ (or whole) step, then release the bend back to the original note. All three notes are tied, only the first note is struck.

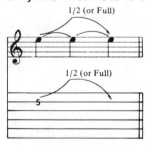

PRE-BEND: Bend the note up ½ (or whole) step, then strike it.

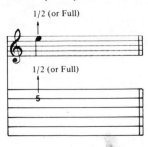

PRE-BEND AND RELEASE: Bend the note up ½ (or whole) step. Strike it and release the bend back to the original note.

UNISON BEND: Strike the two notes simultaneously and bend the lower note up to the pitch of the higher.

VIBRATO: The string is vibrated by rapidly bending and releasing the note with the left hand or tremolo bar.

WIDE OR EXAGGERATED VIBRATO: The pitch is varied to a greater degree by vibrating with the left hand or tremolo bar.

SLIDE: Strike the first note and then slide the same left-hand finger up or down to the second note. The second note is not struck.

SLIDE: Same as above, except the second note is struck.

SLIDE: Slide up to the note indicated from a few frets below.

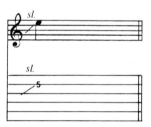

SLIDE: Strike the note and slide up or down an indefinite number of frets, releasing finger pressure at the end of the slide.

PICK SLIDE: The edge of the pick is rubbed down the length of the string producing a scratchy sound.

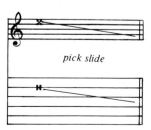

HAMMER-ON: Strike the first (lower) note, then sound the higher note with another finger by fretting it without picking.

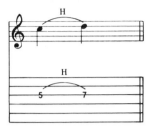

HAMMER-ON: Without picking, sound the note indicated by sharply fretting the note with a left-hand finger.

PULL-OFF: Place both fingers on the notes to be sounded. Strike the first note and without picking, pull the finger off to sound the second (lower) note.

TRILL: Very rapidly alternate between the note indicated and the small note shown is parentheses by hammering on and pulling off.

TAPPING: Hammer ("tap") the fret indicated with the right-hand index or middle finger and pull off to the note fretted by the left hand.

TREMOLO PICKING: The note is picked as rapidly and continuously as possible.

RAKE: Drag the pick across the strings indicated from low to high with a single downward motion.

ARPEGGIO: Play the notes of the chord indicated by quickly rolling them from bottom to top.

NATURAL HARMONIC: Strike the note while the left hand lightly touches the string over the fret indicated.

ARTIFICIAL HARMONIC: The note is fretted normally and a harmonic is produced by adding the edge of the thumb or the tip of the index finger of the right hand to the normal pick attack. High volume or distortion will allow for a greater variety of harmonics.

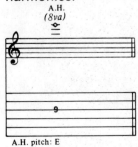

TREMOLO BAR: The pitch of the note or chord is dropped a specified number of steps then returned to the original pitch.

PALM MUTING: The note is partially muted by the right hand lightly touching the string(s) just before the bridge.

MUFFLED STRINGS: A percussive sound is produced by laying the left hand across the strings without depressing them and striking them with the right hand.

RHYTHM SLASHES: Strum chords in rhythm indicated. Use chord voicings found in the fingering diagrams at the top of the first page of the transcription.

RHYTHM SLASHES (SINGLE NOTES): Single notes can be indicated in rhythm slashes. The circled number above the note name indicates which string to play. When successive notes are played on the same string, only the fret numbers are given.

Definitions of Musical Symbols

8va	Play an octave higher than written
15ma	Play two octaves higher than written
loco	Play as written
pp *(pianissimo)*	Very soft
p *(piano)*	Soft
mp *(mezzo - piano)*	Moderately soft
mf *(mezzo - forte)*	Moderately loud
f *(forte)*	Loud
ff *(fortissimo)*	Very loud
> *(accent)*	Accentuate note (play it louder)
^ *(accent)*	Accentuate note with great intensity
· *(staccato)*	Play note short
/	Repeat previous beat (used for quarter or eighth notes)
//	Repeat previous beat (used for sixteenth notes)
./.	Repeat previous measure
‖: :‖	Repeat measures between repeat signs
‖: │ :‖ │ (1. 2. endings)	When a repeated section has different endings, play the first ending only the first time and the second ending only the second time.
D.S. al Coda	Go back to the sign (𝄋), then play until the measure marked "To Coda," then skip to the section labeled "Coda."
D.C. al Fine	Go back to the beginning of the song and play until the measure marked "Fine" (end).

NOTE: Tablature numbers in parentheses mean:

1. The note is being sustained over a barline (note in standard notation is tied), or

2. The note is sustained, but a new articulation (such as a hammer-on, pull-off, slide or vibrato) begins, or

3. The note is a barely audible "ghost" note (note in standard notation is also in parentheses).

POUNDCAKE

Words and Music by
Edward Van Halen, Alex Van Halen,
Michael Anthony and Sammy Hagar

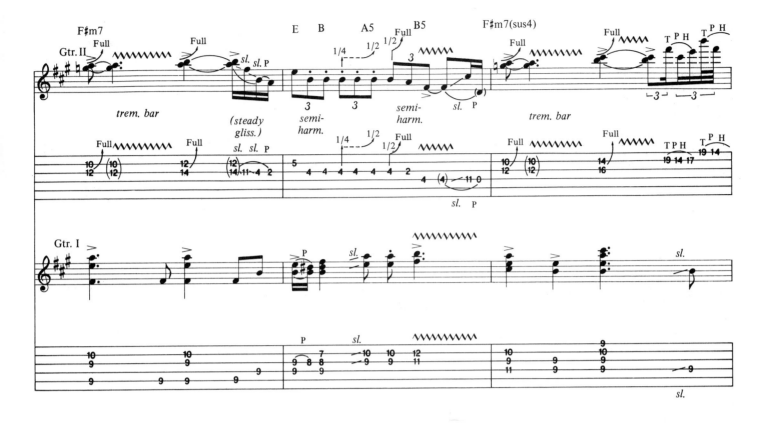

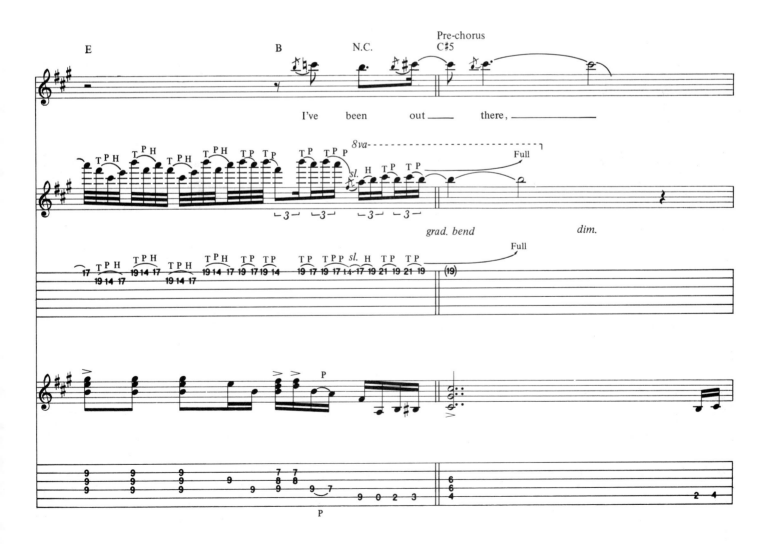

I've been out ___ there, ___

*Two gtrs. One gtr. allows chords to sustain while other plays harmonics.

JUDGEMENT DAY

Words and Music by
Edward Van Halen, Alex Van Halen,
Michael Anthony and Sammy Hagar

SPANKED

Words and Music by
Edward Van Halen, Alex Van Halen,
Michael Anthony and Sammy Hagar

**Eddie actually plays a hybrid gtr./bass doubleneck;
two parts have been arr. for one gtr. in standard
tuning (Gtr. III) for this intro.

*Chords implied by bass.
**At this point, the treble neck of Eddie's hybrid guitar is notated
as Gtr. III, and the bass neck is notated as Gtr. IV, arr. for a normal gtr.
in standard tuning.

Huh!

Gtr. V (clean elec.)

(Gtr. IV)

1st, 2nd Verses

1. A - both feet up, watch - in' T – V,   a-some place to feast my eyes,___   oh___ uh.
2. *See additional lyrics*

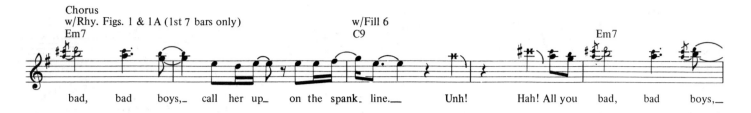

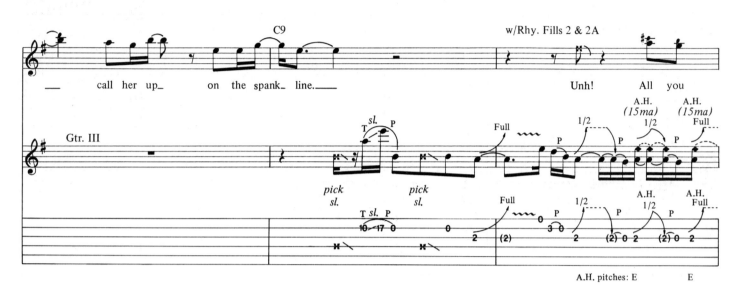

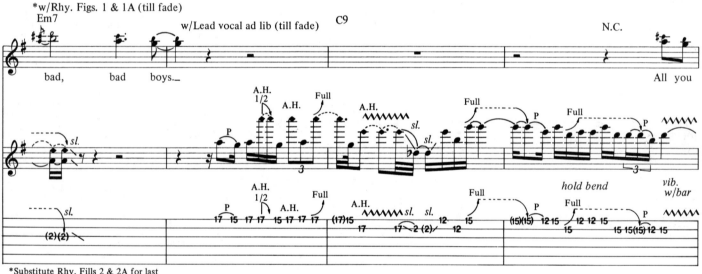

*Substitute Rhy. Fills 2 & 2A for last
bar of Rhy. Figs. 1 & 1A till fade.

*Depress bar before striking note. ** Pull bar up.

*Slide tapping finger off fretboard.

Additional Lyrics

2. Three dollars, first minute,
   After that, cost ya four.
   She be up for negotiations,
   If you call back for more.

2nd Pre-chorus:
Now, who ya gonna call
When ya need that special little somethin'?
You can say what you like,
It's all confidential. *(To Chorus)*

RUNAROUND

Words and Music by
Edward Van Halen, Alex Van Halen,
Michael Anthony and Sammy Hagar

Rhy. Fig. 2

A5   1st Verse

She don't like it when it's cut and dried.___   And don't_like me mak-ing

(end Rhy. Fig. 2)

fu -ture plans.___   And don't_want me try-in' to pin her down.___   She ain't a - bout to give an

w/Rhy. Fig. 2
N.C.(A5)   A5

inch of ground,___ now.___   **Whoo!**___   Well,___

I've got her in my sight,__ but just__ out of reach, oh.____

Chorus
w/Rhy. Fig. 1

Here__ we go a - round.
(Round, a - round,__ a - round.)
Run,__ run,__

run - a - round,____ yeah. Here__ we go a - round.
(Round, a - round,__ a - round, a - round.) (Round, a - round,__ a - round.)

She's giv - in' me the run - a - round,____ yeah,____ oh.
(Round, a - round,__ a - round, a - round.)

*Depress bar before striking note.

PLEASURE DOME

Words and Music by
Edward Van Halen, Alex Van Halen,
Michael Anthony and Sammy Hagar

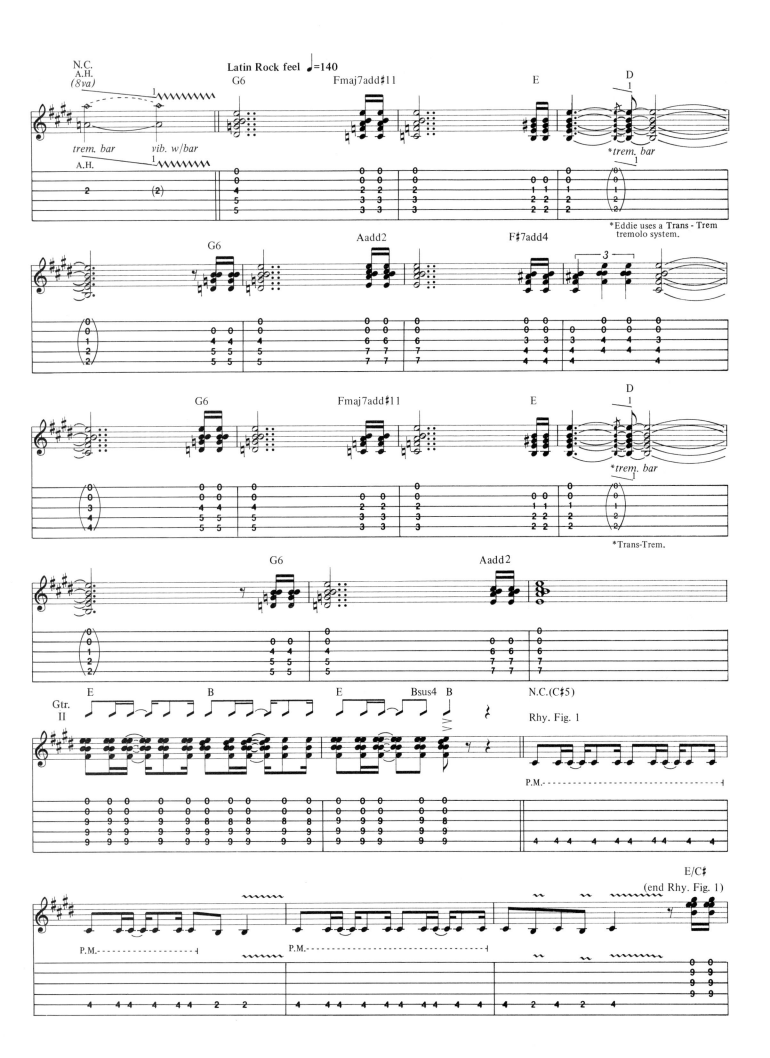

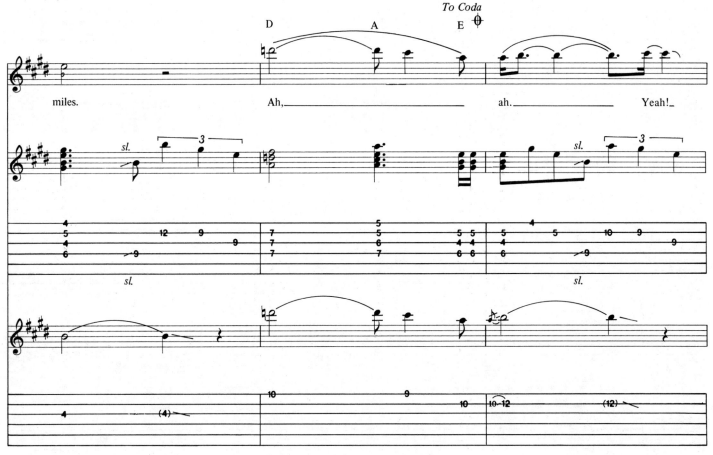

IN 'N' OUT

Words and Music by
Edward Van Halen, Alex Van Halen,
Michael Anthony and Sammy Hagar

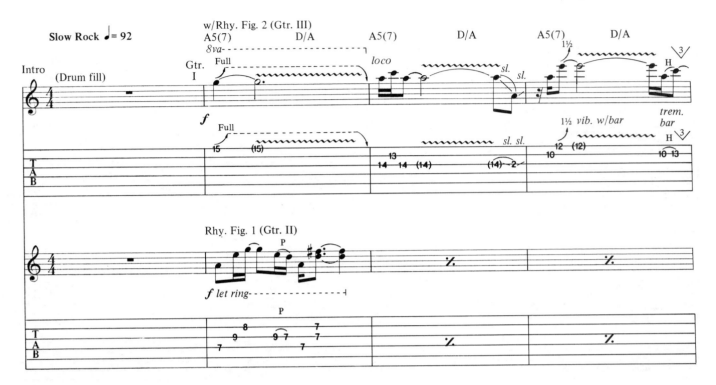

got ya com-in' in.   When they got ya com-in' out.   Got ya com-in' in   for the

Additional Lyrics

2. There ain't no way 'round the system.
Money makes the world go around.
All the way they got you down.
Say you had enough, wanna throw yourself out a window, oh.
Might cost you less to stick around.
One more payment will lay you down, underground.
Well, they got ya comin' in. They got ya goin' out.
Same amount. Woo! In 'n' out. *(To Guitar solo)*

3. Hey, it all depends how you see it.
It's a burden or an opportunity.
One thing for certain, you get nothin' free, uh.
I've never met a man doesn't owe somebody somethin', no.
No way to get free and clear.
Oh, in deeper, year after year, oh yeah.
When they got ya comin' in. When they got ya goin' out. *(etc.)*

MAN ON A MISSION

Words and Music by
Edward Van Halen, Alex Van Halen,
Michael Anthony and Sammy Hagar

*Flick trem. bar to produce flutter.

*Tapped harmonics

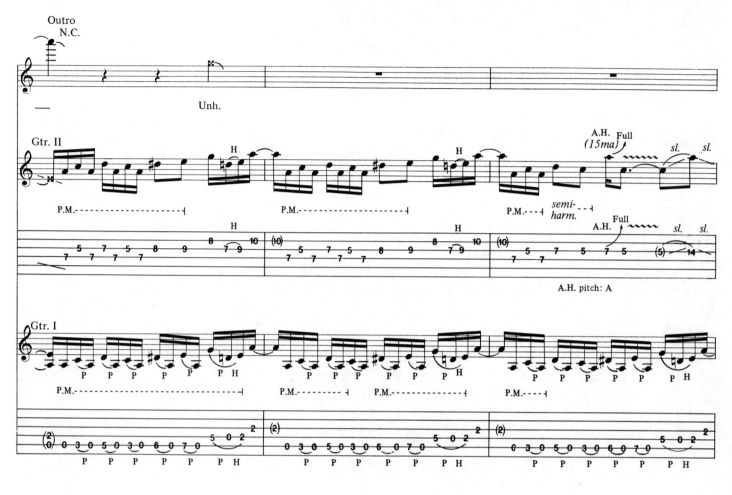

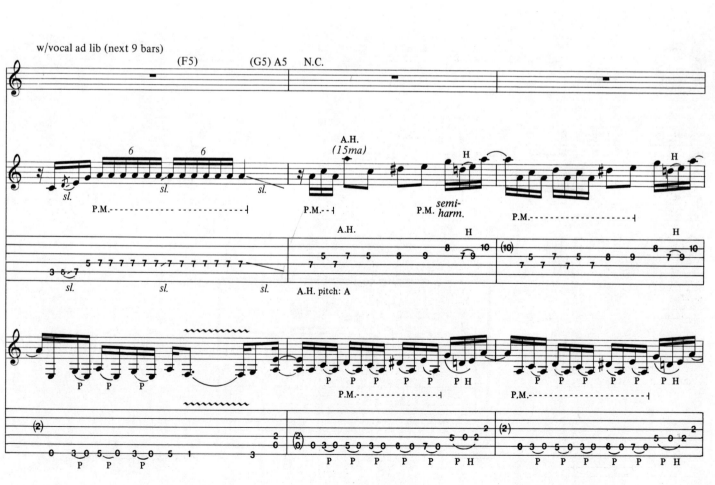

Additional Lyrics

2. You give every inch: flesh, blood and bone.
   And it's all wrapped up in a tight little bundle.
   I got an open mind. Do anything,
   Anywhere the ball might roll or tumble.

2nd Pre-chorus:
Right down to the bottom or the top,
I'm gonna get it all in one big pop.
Yeah, she got, she got me hot! *(To Chorus)*

THE DREAM IS OVER

Words and Music by
Edward Van Halen, Alex Van Halen,
Michael Anthony and Sammy Hagar

316

Music by Edward Van Halen, Alex Van Halen,
Michael Anthony and Sammy Hagar

*Tapped harmonics.

RIGHT NOW

Words and Music by
Edward Van Halen, Alex Van Halen,
Michael Anthony and Sammy Hagar

1. Don't wan - na wait_ till to - mor - row,   why put it off   an-oth - er day?_
2. *See additional lyrics*

One by   one,   girl,   prob - lems ___   build up_

___   and stand   in our way.___   Oh!

One_ step a - head,_ one_ step be - hind_

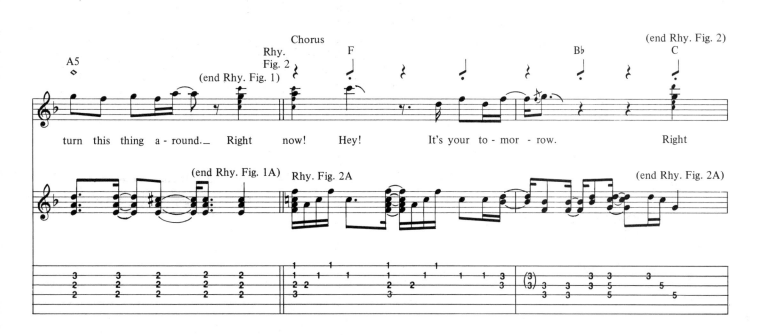

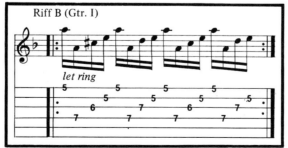

Additional Lyrics

2. Miss a beat, you lose the rhythm
   And nothing falls into place.
   Only missed by a fraction,
   Sent a little off your pace.

2nd Pre-chorus:
The more things you get, the more you want.
Just tradin' one for the other.
Workin' so hard to make it easy.
Got to turn, come on, turn this thing around. *(To Chorus)*

TOP OF THE WORLD

Words and Music by
Edward Van Halen, Alex Van Halen,
Michael Anthony and Sammy Hagar

See the whole___ wide___ world turn___ up - side down.___ ___
___ oo.___ Oo, oo.___ Oo, oo.)___

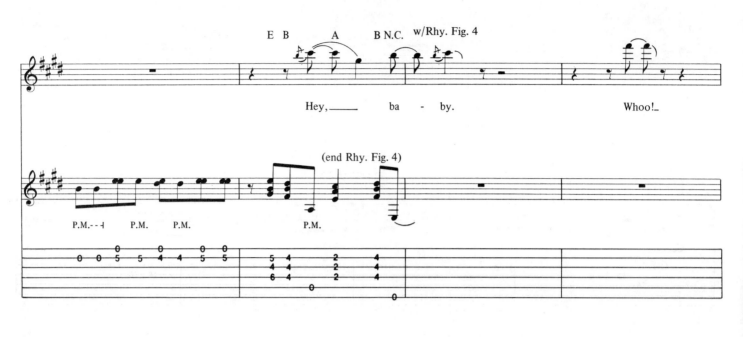

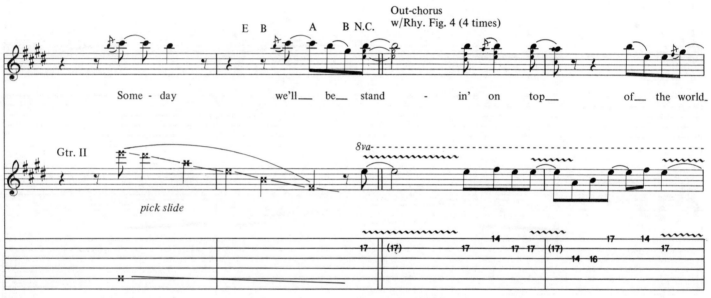

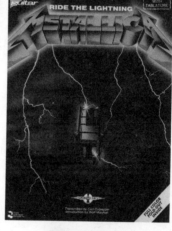

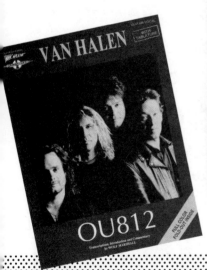

SPEND A YEAR WITH

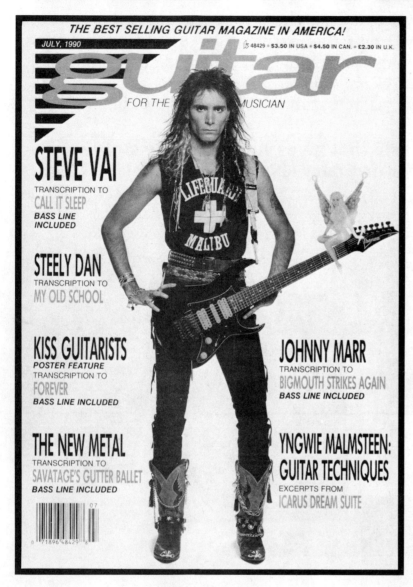

THE BEST SELLING GUITAR MAGAZINE IN AMERICA!

JULY, 1990

guitar FOR THE ... MUSICIAN

$3.50 IN USA • $4.50 IN CAN. • £2.30 IN U.K.

STEVE VAI
TRANSCRIPTION TO
CALL IT SLEEP
BASS LINE INCLUDED

STEELY DAN
TRANSCRIPTION TO
MY OLD SCHOOL

KISS GUITARISTS
POSTER FEATURE
TRANSCRIPTION TO
FOREVER
BASS LINE INCLUDED

THE NEW METAL
TRANSCRIPTION TO
SAVATAGE'S GUTTER BALLET
BASS LINE INCLUDED

JOHNNY MARR
TRANSCRIPTION TO
BIGMOUTH STRIKES AGAIN
BASS LINE INCLUDED

**YNGWIE MALMSTEEN:
GUITAR TECHNIQUES**
EXCERPTS FROM
ICARUS DREAM SUITE

Eddie Van Halen
Steve Vai
Randy Rhoads
Yngwie Malmsteen
Jimi Hendrix
Vinnie Moore
Stevie Ray Vaughan
Guns N' Roses
Jeff Watson
Carlos Santana
Neal Schon
Eric Clapton
Jimmy Page
Jake E. Lee
Brad Gillis
George Lynch
Metallica
Keith Richards
Jeff Beck
Michael Schenker ...

AND SAVE $14.00 off the newsstand price!

Just $27.95 buys you a year's subscription to GUITAR and the chance to spend 12 months studying the techniques and the artistry of the world's best guitar performers.

Get started ... mail the coupon below!

Every issue of GUITAR gives you:

• sheet music you can't get anywhere else—with accurate transcriptions of the original artists.

• in-depth interviews with guitar greats who candidly discuss the nuts and bolts of what they do.

• columns and articles on the music, the equipment and the techniques that are making waves.

Become a better guitarist and performer. Study with the professionals every month in GUITAR FOR THE PRACTICING MUSICIAN.

To start your subscription — *and save 33% off the cover price* — write GUITAR P.O. Box 53063, Boulder, CO 80322-3063